The Walking With God

"Follow Me!"
Walking With Jesus in Everyday Life

Don Cousins & Judson Poling

Zondervan Publishing House
Grand Rapids, Michigan

A Division of HarperCollinsPublishers

The Walking With God Series

Friendship With God:
  Developing Intimacy With God

The Incomparable Jesus:
  Experiencing the Power of Christ

"Follow Me!":
  Walking With Jesus in Everyday Life

Discovering the Church:
  Becoming Part of God's New Community

Building Your Church:
  Using Your Gifts, Time, and Resources

Impacting Your World:
  Becoming a Person of Influence

Published by Zondervan Publishing House, Grand Rapids, Michigan 49530
Produced by The Livingstone Corporation. James C. Galvin, J. Michael Kendrick, Daryl J. Lucas, and Darcy J. Kamps, project staff.

ISBN 0-310-59163-5

Cover design: Mark Veldheer
Interior design: Catherine Bergstrom

Printed in the United States of America
  93 94 95 96 97 98 99 / DP / 9 8 7 6 5 4 3

Preface

The *Walking With God Series* was developed as the curriculum for small groups at Willow Creek Community Church in South Barrington, Illinois. This innovative church has grown to over 15,000 in less than two decades, and the material here flows out of the vision and values of this dynamic ministry. Groups using these studies have produced many of the leaders, both staff and volunteer, throughout the church.

Associate Pastor Don Cousins wrote the first draft of this material and used it with his own small group. After testing it there, he revised it and passed his notes to Judson Poling, Director of Curriculum Development, who edited and expanded the outlines. Several pilot groups helped shape the material as it was being written and revised. A team of leaders labored through a line-by-line revision of these study guides over a year's span of time. Finally, these revisions were put into this new, more usable format.

Any church or group can use these studies in a relational context to help raise up devoted disciples. Group members who finish all six books will lay a solid foundation for a lifelong walk with God.

Willow Creek Resources is a publishing partnership between Zondervan Publishing House and the Willow Creek Association. Willow Creek Resources will include drama sketches, small group curricula, training material, videos, and many other specialized ministry resources.

Willow Creek Association is an international network of churches ministering to the unchurched. Founded in 1992, the Willow Creek Association serves churches through conferences, seminars, regional roundtables, consulting, and ministry resource materials. The mission of the Association is to assist churches in reestablishing the priority and practice of reaching lost people for Christ through church ministries targeted to seekers.

For conference and seminar information please write to:

Willow Creek Association
P.O. Box 3188
Barrington, Illinois 60011-3188

Contents

"Follow Me!"

Walking With Jesus in Everyday Life

Introduction

Salvation is described by the Scriptures as a free gift. Yet Jesus also spoke of discipleship as costly, and urged those who would follow him to count the cost. For Jesus, no final conflict existed between receiving his gracious forgiveness and following his exacting lordship. He knew that as Savior he was offering something to sinful people that they couldn't earn, yet as their Lord he was calling them to a life of service which required obedience at every turn. The concept of receiving the gift without deference to the Giver was unthinkable.

To take part in the relationship ("Savior" and "Forgiver") without embracing *all* Jesus is ("Master" and "Leader") would be as ridiculous as going through a marriage ceremony without anticipating a lifetime of loving and serving your spouse. Technically, you don't become married just by acting like you're married, and you don't become a Christian by living a good life, but would it make any sense to become married with no intention of acting like it? Does it make sense to receive Christ without responding daily in obedience to his commands?

Ephesians 2:8-9 promises us unconditional grace that saves us; the very next verse (2:10) tells us that God prepared good works for us to walk in them. In this book, we will examine in greater detail what it means to follow Christ as Lord day by day. This will bring you and your group members to a point where you can identify areas for personal growth and what, in particular, what you need to do to make the lordship of Christ more functional in your lives.

Follow Me . . . I'll Protect You

PURPOSE

A small child was once asked to sit down in the car. "I can't drive until you sit and buckle your seat belt," said the mother.

"No," replied the child.

"I will tell you again—sit down and buckle your belt."

"No," was the defiant answer.

"You either sit down and obey me, or we'll both get out of the car and I'll spank you!" responded the exasperated mother.

The child just glared at her silently. As the mother began to open the car door to make good on her threat, the child immediately sat down and buckled the belt.

"That's better," said the mother.

As they began to drive off, the child said under his breath but loud enough to be heard, "I may be sitting down on the outside, but I'm standing up on the inside."

This story illustrates several important concepts about obedience. First, obedience maintains interpersonal harmony, while its opposite—disobedience—causes conflicts. When someone disobeys an authority, friction occurs between the two. Second, when the person issuing directives does the right thing, obedience is for our well-being. Third, obedience is not the same as mere conformity to someone else's wishes. How often are we "standing up on the inside" even though we're "sitting down on the outside!" True obedience is done willingly out of trust in the one with authority; conformity is merely begrudging adjustment of our outward actions.

In this study we will explore what it means to obey Christ.

What Is Obedience?

What does it mean to have authority?

Authority is having the ability to persuade or control someone or a group

In what ways do you respond or have you responded to the authority of:

the government?

obedient - its expected in society

a parent?

more rebellious

a coach?

if encouraging - very respondant

the church?

- very obedient until I became more aware of things going on

What does it mean in practical (rather than theological) terms to call Jesus "Lord"?
(Luke 6:46) To do what he says and listen to his will

What does our level of obedience to God show us? (John 14:15)

When we obey - it shows how deeply we love him

14

Who does Jesus say are his "brothers and sisters"? (Matthew 12:47-50)

Whoever does the will of the father

Why Is Obedience to God So Important?

What effect does our obedience have on God? (1 Thessalonians 4:1-2)

it pleases him

In what ways does obedience protect us?

Psalm 32:3-7

from sin + guilt

Psalm 119:45

freedom

Romans 1:27

from unnatural relations

How has obedience to God protected you?

God has protected me from all the common falling grounds like drinking smoking etc - He's protected me bt a family that cares

What effect does obedience and disobedience have on our conscience?

Ephesians 4:18-19

Our hearts arent hardened - we can ask forgiveness - lust hasnt taken over

1 Timothy 1:19

Obedience produces faith which allows us w/ a clean conscious

1 Timothy 4:2

leaves hypocrites

How has God's Word influenced your behavior in an area that otherwise probably wouldn't matter to you? My purity — I have a tendency to want physical satisfaction - w/out Gods wnds and promises to those who stay pure- I probably wouldnt be

According to the following verses, what different effects can obedience to God have on our relationships with others?

Luke 6:22-23

- Some could hate you because of it

Luke 6:27-28

mistreatment

When has your obedience to God negatively impacted a personal relationship?

When someone I felt I could be a very close to needed some space and I need some time to obey God - I lost that relationship because I was obedient to what God wants

When have you chosen to respond with kindness toward someone who has mistreated me to d *you for being a Christian?*

I guess when Trupti and I would talk- she never really mistreated me as such but it was hard

---

BOTTOM LINE

Bible

Schedule three times this week to get alone with God. Pick times during the day that work best for you. Each time, read 1 Peter 1, noting observations and applications.

Prayer

Day One: Adoration—List ten ways God has shown his faithfulness to you.

Day Two: Confession—Review the last two days and write out a prayer of confession.

Day Three: Thanksgiving—Give thanks to God for three qualities in your spouse or a close friend. Then tell that person about what you were thankful for.

Scripture Memory

As part of the curriculum, we've included memory verses with each study. If you want to make this discipline part of your discipleship experience, begin by memorizing this verse:

Why do you call me, "Lord, Lord," and do not do what I say?   Luke 6:46

Next week we will explore what it means to obey Christ in the "gray areas" of life. To prepare for the study, think about how you determine what is right and wrong for you when there are no specific commands about the issue in Scripture. What principles have you found useful for making decisions in these situations?

1) basic needs
2) providing open doors when I think all are closed
3) comforting me in depression/sorrow
4) giving me a good roommate, friends, family,
5) answering my prayers with Wait or No - He knows what best for me
6) Allowing me to grow spiritually with him <
7) Keeps his promise that I will be provide for in _all_ my needs -
8) Gives me endurance and hope. 17
9) Builds up my confidence and self esteem
10) Saved me when I repented of my sins and looked to Jesus

Follow Me . . .
I'll Direct You

PURPOSE

Lately your boss has been pressuring you to put in excessive overtime hours. You've been talking with him about Christ and feel a heightened responsibility to live rightly. You wonder: Should you submit to your boss's pressure to work at this hectic pace?

Your daughter, meanwhile, has been invited to the prom by a non-Christian guy. She is seventeen, and you want to give her the right amount of freedom without letting her make a poor decision. To what extent should you intervene as she decides whether to accept?

On the way home from work, you're reminded that your car is getting old and on the brink of falling apart. Sometime soon you will need to replace it. As a Christian, does it matter what kind of car you get or how much you spend on it?

Most of what we do in life is not regulated by specific commands of Scripture. We work, go to school, shop, and do many other activities that require us to use our judgment. How can we be sure of always making the right choices? What does it mean to obey Christ in the "gray" areas?

In this study, we will examine four steps we can use to help us obey God in any area of life.

Four Questions for Evaluating Our Actions

1 Is it beneficial in any way?

What are some examples of some activities that may be permissible but not necessarily beneficial? (1 Corinthians 6:12)

— I guess those things that are over done
— drinking, smoking, driving too fast etc
— sweets

What is something that is permissible to some but not beneficial for you?

— smoking
— drinking

Can you think of a time recently that you participated in something that later you wish you hadn't because it wasn't profitable?

Writing that check to Alcohol Liquor Outlet

2 Does it master me?

What are some activities that could master a person? (1 Corinthians 6:12)

overeating, sex, drinking etc etc
Money, gambling

What activities do you need to guard against becoming master over you?

eating sweets
Kissing
studies

3 Could it hurt someone else's walk with God?

Why should we limit our freedom? (1 Corinthians 10:24)

Because it could be offensive to someone else

How could a neutral or permissible activity hurt someone else? (1 Corinthians 8:13)

They might not agree w/it, therefore hurts our witness to do it

4 Does it glorify God?

What does it mean to glorify God? (1 Corinthians 10:31)

Doing everything for the glory of God — do not allow yourself to let someone stumble

How can everyday actions (like eating and drinking) bring glory to God?

Maybe if you eat w/someone besides your group in the cafe or something

---

BOTTOM LINE

Do everything for the glory of God — The decisions we make because we have freedom should be through prayer and faith

Bible

Read Matthew 16 three times.

Prayer

Day One: Adoration—Read Psalm 135 in an attitude of prayer.

Day Two: Confession—Identify a sin you struggle with regularly. Try to find a verse that speaks directly to that sin. Meditate on that verse.

Day Three: Thanksgiving—Thank God for who he made you—physically, relationally, mentally, and emotionally. Be specific in your prayer.

Scripture Memory

So whether you eat or drink or whatever you do, do it all for the glory of God.   1 Corinthians 10:31

3

Jesus, Lord of Who I Am

In the hearts of countless Americans, few events are more fascinating than a romance between celebrities. The press eagerly snatches up every details of the courtship and reports them to a fascinated public. The couple makes orchestrated public appearances, exuding radiant smiles and tender looks for one another as the photographers take picture after picture. Finally they announce wedding plans, vowing that their relationship will last forever. The ceremony is a lavish spectacle, attended by admiring peers and surrounded by fans who hope to catch a glimpse of their idols. Yes, this must be love . . . or is it?

Soon, disturbing stories of discord between the couple emerge. They are seen less frequently together, and soon it becomes evident that the fairy-tale romance has lost its magic. Rumors circulate that both partners are seeing other people. Within a year, the stories are borne out by an announcement of a pending divorce. Recriminations fly between the couple in the press, and reporters find fresh copy digging up the details about new relationships that each partner has begun. Why do so many romances among the famous (and not-so-famous) end in disaster?

One obvious answer might be that people fail to perceive the commitment necessary to maintain a relationship. It is easy to make that first step, to pledge lifelong devotion to another person. Yet when problems and conflicts happen, it requires self-sacrifice and hard work to make those commitments stick. Our Christian lives also require that kind of devotion if we are to remain effective servants for God. In this study, you will gain an understanding of what it means to be a disciple of the *Lord* Jesus Christ, submitted to his lordship.

The key verse for this study is Matthew 16:24—*"Then Jesus said to his disciples, 'If anyone would come after me, he must deny himself and take up his cross and follow me.'"*

If you were with the disciples when Jesus said this, how might you have reacted?

They might not have realized what the cross was

Deny Self

What does it mean to deny self?

To deny self is to not give in to all our own selfish wants and desires and to be more open to others needs, how we can help others

What should we deny or say no to?

The things we want - our own desires

In what area has it been hard for you to deny yourself lately?

sweets - I don't know - depression - self pity

Take Up Your Cross

What did it mean for a person to literally take up a cross in Jesus' day?

to die on cross

What truth about walking with God was Jesus trying to communicate when he said take up your cross?

that we have to deny ourselves

Why is it uncomfortable or unnatural for each of us to take up our cross?

I think because we naturally think of ourselves on most occasions

Why is it important to take up your cross daily?

How does taking up your cross relate to family life?

Follow Christ

What are some other words that mean the same as "follow"?

In what ways do you find it easy to imitate Jesus?

In what ways is it difficult to imitate Jesus?

In what area of life do you want to become more like Jesus? How?

BOTTOM LINE

Following Jesus means denying sin and dying to its pleasure in order to glorify God

YOUR WALK WITH GOD

Bible

Study Matthew 19, especially 19:16-26, "The Rich Young Man."

Prayer

Day One: Adoration—Paraphrase Psalm 139:1-6 as a prayer of adoration to God. Come up with a title for this part of the psalm.

Day Two: Confession—On three separate occasions during the week, look back over the previous day's events and conversations to identify anything you need to confess.

Day Three: Thanksgiving—Thank God for what God has done for you.

Scripture Memory

Then Jesus said to his disciples, "If anyone would come after me, he must deny himself and take up his cross and follow me." Matthew 16:24

In the next study we will take a look at what it means for Jesus as lord of what we have. To prepare, think about the possessions you would most hate to lose.

4

Jesus, Lord of What I Have

To those who knew him, the rich young man had no money problem. He had power, comfort, and prestige. Every material need he had was easily met. Yet something inside him sensed that he still needed something else to be truly satisfied. He came to Jesus hoping for affirmation and comfort. But when Jesus exposed the source of his restlessness, the ruler balked. He probably could have made any other sacrifice, but being required to surrender his wealth was too threatening, for it was the foundation of his security. His money problem was not a lack of means, but rather an excessive dependence on it.

Christians sometimes have the same struggles as the rich young man. Reliance on wealth can create bondage and anxiety for believers as well as for nonbelievers. But a big part of being Christ's disciple is handling your resources in a way that honors God. That's a tough challenge. In this study you will learn a way to meet that challenge.

STUDY

Rich Young Man

What various details do we know about the man who came to see Jesus? (Matthew 19:16-26)

was rich, young

27

What did Jesus accomplish by his response to the young man's question? (Matthew 19:17)

wealth wasnt the way

Why do you think Jesus listed the commandments he did? (Matthew 19:18-19)

He was starting w/ broad spectrum going straight to the man

Why did the man insist that he still lacked something? (Matthew 19:20-21)

He didnt think it was that simple

According to Jesus, what was the man's problem? (Matthew 19:21)

He had too many earthly treasures

Why did Jesus say that it is hard for rich people to enter the kingdom of heaven? (Matthew 19:23-24)

Because its hard to give up those riches for something unknown

Why were the disciples so incredulous at Jesus' comments? (Matthew 19:25-26)

What do you most want to remember about Jesus' talk with the rich young man?

The fact that we need to put our heads and treasures aside to Him

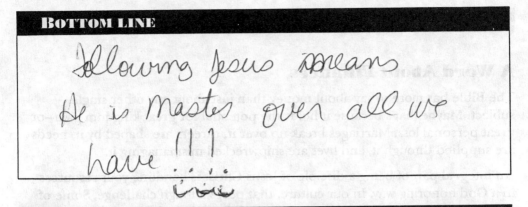

Following Jesus means
He is Master over all we
have !!!

Bible

Read Matthew 20 three times, noting observations and applications.

Prayer

Day One: Adoration—Paraphrase Psalm 139:7-12 and pray through it. Come up with a title for this part of the psalm.

Day Two: Supplication—List two or three sins you would especially like to defeat in your life. Ask God to replace these with characteristics of his.

Day Three: Thanksgiving—Thank God for one thing or person you've taken for granted lately.

Scripture Memory

Review the memory verses you have learned so far in *"Follow Me!"*: Luke 6:46; 1 Corinthians 10:31; and Matthew 16:24.

In the next study we will take a look at some of the benefits of following Jesus. What do you value most about your relationship with God? What "nice extras" have you experienced that you did not expect when you first became a Christian?

A Word About Finances

The Bible has more to say about money than just about any other single subject. Maybe that's because it holds the potential for great kingdom gain—or great personal loss. Marriages break up over it, careers are shaped by it, needs are supplied through it, and lives are shipwrecked mismanaging it.

An integral part of being a disciple of Jesus Christ is handling your resources in a God-honoring way. In our culture, that poses a tough challenge. Some of you may be like the rich young man in tonight's study and do not yet recognize your obeisance and obedience to another god. Or you may tend to the opposite extreme: always longing but never having. You may worship the same god as the rich young man, only you do so from a distance. Many will be somewhere in the middle. Whatever your situation, it is important to note: *Proper money management—stewardship—is essential for a mature follower of Jesus Christ.*

Jesus, Lord of All

Have you ever signed up for a "free offer" only to find out you were going to be billed $19.95 for it? Perhaps you were one of the lucky winners of a "free gift" only to find out you had to listen to a two hour sales pitch to claim it. "There's no such thing as a free lunch," as the saying goes. You pay a price for almost everything. This is as true of following Christ as it is in any other area of life.

The last two studies went into detail about the costs of being a disciple of Christ. Those costs are: (1) deny yourself, (2) take up your cross, (3) follow Christ, (4) submit all you have to the Lord. It is not hard to see from that list that the cost is substantial.

But the cost is also worth paying. Jesus didn't hold back from telling his disciples of the benefits of following him. In this study you'll learn about those benefits.

STUDY

What are the costs of following Christ?

- guving up your boyfriend
- Struggling with ativation   - having pure
- feeling burdened   - feeling accomplishment
- receiving blessing
- feeling joy

31

What did you have to give up to become a Christian?

Not a lot — I was five so really nothing. To maintain Christian attitudes I'm sure I had to give up some things but it never seemed like I was

Benefits of Following Christ

(1) God's Provision

What benefit did Jesus promise to all who seek his kingdom first? (Matthew 6:33)

All these things will be added unto you Allelua Alleluia

(2) Freedom

What benefit is there in believing the truth about Christ? (John 8:32)

The truth will let us free
we will feel the love and peace + joy that comes from the truth

(3) Peace of Mind

In what kinds of circumstances does Jesus promise us peace of mind? (John 14:27)

(4) Joy

What is unique about Jesus' joy? (John 15:11)

(5) Peace with God

What is peace with God? (Romans 5:1-2)

6 God's Love

How did God show his love for us? (Romans 5:5-8)

7 Hope of Heaven

What does the future hold for those without the hope of heaven? (Romans 5:9-10)

8 Character Development

How does God change our character? (Romans 8:28-29)

9 Access to God

What assurance do we have about our prayers? (Hebrews 4:16)

Conclusion

Why is it worth paying the costs of following Christ? (1 Corinthians 9:24-27)

If you had to single out only one, which of these benefits would you select as the most meaningful to you?

YOUR WALK WITH GOD

Bible

Read and study Matthew 21 three times. As you read, let these two questions guide your observations and applications: (1) In what way were these events the "beginning of the end" for Jesus? (2) What do you learn about Jesus from this chapter?

Prayer

Day One: Adoration—Paraphrase Psalm 139:13-18 and pray through it.

Day Two: Confession—On three separate occasions, focus on the previous day's events and let the Holy Spirit convict you of whatever sins need cleansing.

Day Three: Thanksgiving—In your prayer, complete the sentence, "Heavenly Father, thank you for the opportunities I have to _____."

Scripture Memory

Everyone who competes in the games goes into strict training. They do it to get a crown that will not last; but we do it to get a crown that will last forever. 1 Corinthians 9:25

In the next study we will take a closer look at the expectations we have for God. Do you expect him to give you a life free from difficulty? Do you sometimes find yourself thinking that God owes you something? What do you expect God to do for you?

The Beginning of the End

Expectations have a way of setting us up for disappointment. Consider, for example, some of the actions you expect from your family or friends—perhaps keeping you informed of their whereabouts, or taking out the trash every Thursday night. Whether these expectations are realistic doesn't matter; you have come to depend on them. What happens when they aren't met?

Palm Sunday was a clash of expectations. Jesus had arrived in Jerusalem six days before the Passover, one of the most important holidays in the Jewish calendar. Thousands of people had crammed into Jerusalem to observe the feast. Shortly before he entered the city, he had raised Lazarus from the dead; when people heard about it, anticipation built for what he would do next. Many people fully expected him to liberate them from Rome. He was greeted by a throng of admiring locals.

But those expectations did not match Jesus' mission. Rather than coming to conquer Rome, he had come to conquer sin; his aims were spiritual, not political. Some sort of letdown was inevitable. And so, when it became clear that Jesus would not use his power for nationalistic ends, popularity swung to the religious leaders. Festive Palm Sunday was, ironically, the beginning of the end for Jesus.

In this study, we will focus on the events of Palm Sunday, one of the key events in God's unfolding plan of salvation.

The Triumphal Entry

How did the crowds greet Jesus as he was riding into the city of Jerusalem? (Matthew 21:1-11)

Why did the crowds gather to greet Jesus? (John 12:9-11, 17-18)

What is the significance of Jesus riding in on a donkey? (Zechariah 9:9)

Why did the crowds say what they did about Jesus? (Matthew 21:9-11)

The Beginning of the End

Nearly a week later, after Jesus had been arrested and tried, the crowd condemned Jesus to die (Matthew 27:15-26). How could Jesus be rejected by the crowd so soon after he was hailed as their king?

We sometimes want God to act in ways that compromise his character. What are some examples of expecting what we shouldn't from God?

When has there been a time when you expected God to act a certain way and he refused?

In what ways do you need to adjust your expectations of God at this point in your life?

How should we adjust our expectations in order to serve God totally? (John 12:24-26)

In what ways are you a means to God's ends today?

When has God used a painful event in your life to accomplish his purposes in or through you?

BOTTOM LINE

Bible

Read Matthew 22–23 three times, noting observations and applications.

Prayer

Day One: Adoration—Paraphrase Psalm 139:19-24 as a prayer of adoration.

Day Two: Supplication—Pray for sensitivity to God's purposes in your life.

Day Three: Thanksgiving—List the purposes God has for your life—all the ones you can think of. Thank him for his care.

Scripture Memory

"For whoever wants to save his life will lose it, but whoever loses his life for me will find it."   Matthew 16:25

In the next study we will take a look at the opposition that Jesus experienced during his ministry. When has your following Christ produced negative reactions in others? How did you respond? What problems or opportunities did this create for you?

Jesus Under Attack

Most people want to be liked by somebody—to feel affirmed, appreciated, important. Who hasn't done something with the hope that "so-and-so will really be pleased"? Whether it be your parents, your boss, the crowd, or a personal mentor, the desire to please can be a great motivator.

But being liked was not at the top of Jesus' priorities. Rather, he did what was right—what the Father wanted him to do—at all costs, and taught others that they should do the same. His healings did gain him many admirers, but he did not heal them to win their favor or to seek their recognition. While the crowds liked him, his hard stand against hypocrisy exposed the religious leaders of his day, and over time Jesus gained more and more enemies. While Jesus knew this, he never altered his deeds or words to halt the defection.

Christians who live their faith openly will encounter opposition too. Those trapped in darkness hate the light. Just as the world rejected Jesus, it will reject those who follow him. Because rejection from the world is inevitable, we should do all we can to prepare for it.

In this study, you will learn how to handle opposition by seeing the way Jesus was opposed and how he responded.

Jesus Under Attack

How did the religious leaders try to trap Jesus? (Matthew 21:23-27; 22:15-46)

Why did the Pharisees and others try to trap Jesus? (Matthew 22:15-46)

Jesus' Response

For what did Jesus condemn the religious leaders? (Matthew 23:1-39)

What can we learn from the Pharisees' negative example?

Conclusion

What sort of opposition does Jesus receive today?

What can you learn from the way Jesus responded to opposition?

Can you think of a time in the past when you experienced opposition for being a Christian?

_____

_____

Why might experiencing opposition be a sign of obedience to God? (2 Timothy 3:12)

_____

_____

In what ways can Christians bring unnecessary criticism and opposition upon themselves?

BOTTOM LINE

YOUR WALK WITH GOD

Bible

Read and study Matthew 24–25 three times.

Prayer

This week, it's your turn to come up with creative prayer ideas! Use the basic A.C.T.S. format, but identify your own specific emphases. Be prepared to share what you did for each next week.

Adoration: _____

Confession: _____

Thanksgiving: _____

Supplication: _____

Scripture Memory

"Blessed are you when men hate you, when they exclude you and insult you and reject your name as evil, because of the Son of Man."   Luke 6:22

In the next study we will learn about Christ's promise to return. What emotions does that event evoke in you?

8

Ready For His Return

We are always getting ready for something. We get ready for bed, for work, for dinner, for retirement. We prepare meals and prepare for dinner guests. The more important the upcoming event, the more time and energy we spend preparing.

Jesus has not finished what he set out to do among us. When Jesus ascended into heaven, he didn't leave this earth permanently. When all other great religious leaders died, they left behind their teachings, their example, their followers, and their corpses. Only Jesus rose—bodily—from the dead. And only Jesus will return—bodily—to earth.

When Jesus does return, he will terminate history as we know it. He will answer all our questions. He will assume his final place as Lord as every knee bows. He will expose and judge all evil deeds. And he will fulfill all of God's promises.

Following Jesus means living in the light of that truth. Not only is our Savior alive, and not only is he with us through the Holy Spirit—he is also coming again!

Be on the Alert for His Coming

What do you observe about the second coming of Christ from Matthew 24:26-35?

In what ways can you ready yourself for Christ's coming?

How can you remind yourself that Jesus will return?

What distracts you from being "on the alert"?

The Two Kinds of Slaves

What do the main characters in this parable represent? (Matthew 24:45-51)

In what ways have you been like each of these slaves?

The Ten Virgins

Who are the main characters in this parable? (Matthew 25:1-13)

How does this parable challenge you?

The Talents

Who are the main characters in the Parable of the Talents? (Matthew 25:14-30)

Where do you need to be more faithful with what God has given to you?

Conclusion

What simple step or activity could you do this week that would help you be more prepared for Christ's coming?

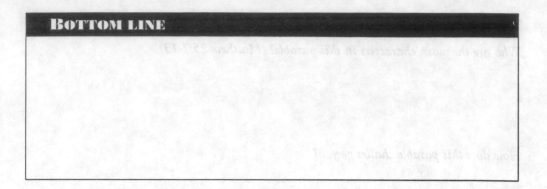

YOUR WALK WITH GOD

Bible

Read and study Matthew 26 three times.

Prayer

Day One: Adoration—During the events described in Matthew 26, right before he died on the cross, Jesus said no to many natural human desires. What were those desires? What other godly attributes did he display in resisting those temptations?

Day Two: Confession—To what selfish desires do you need to die in order to live for God?

Day Three: Supplication—Pray for God to help you die to the desires you listed.

Scripture Memory

Review the following memory verses: 1 Corinthians 9:25; Matthew 16:25; and Luke 6:22.

Next study is about Jesus being betrayed and his commitment to doing the Father's will. What about God's will do you struggle with? What does it mean to pray "your will be done"?

9

Betrayed!

Life is hard. Beside its joys and rewards come difficulties and disappointments. And getting older often means taking on more of life's burdens, not fewer of them. "What a heavy burden God has laid on men!" (Ecclesiastes 1:13).

Jesus' life was no different. In fact, his very mission was to suffer and die—unjustly. The price he paid—separation from God—cost him more than we can imagine. His suffering was intense not just while he was on the cross, but even before, as in the Garden of Gethsemane he faced the certainty of the pain he would suffer.

Yet Jesus willingly went through with his mission. Why? Because he wanted to do his Father's will more than anything else. His agonizing prayer, "Not as I will, but as you will" (Matthew 26:39), was not just a prayer. It was his life and mission.

This study takes you through the final preparations by Judas and the chief priests to arrest Jesus, and climaxes at the point in Jesus' trial where Peter denies him. It is a dismal chapter but as such, it is full of important warnings No can ever safely consider himself or herself bulletproof against the attacks of Satan. Rather, our prayer must perpetually be, "not as I will, but as you will."

Jesus' Final Hours

Matthew 26 describes eight separate incidents in Jesus' final hours of life on earth. They are:

1. The plot to kill Jesus (Matthew 26:1-5)

2. The costly perfume controversy (Matthew 26:6-13)

3. Judas arranges to betray Jesus (Matthew 26:14-16)

4. The Last Supper (Matthew 26:17-30)

5. The Garden of Gethsemane (Matthew 26:31-46)

6. The betrayal and arrest of Jesus (Matthew 26:47-56)

7. Jesus' trial before Caiaphas (Matthew 26:57-68)

8. Peter's denial (Matthew 26:69-75)

1 The plot to kill Jesus

Why did the Jewish religious leaders plot to kill Jesus? (Matthew 26:1-5)

In what way is Jesus' lordship a threat to our authority over ourselves?

2 The costly perfume controversy

Why did Jesus defend the woman for pouring expensive perfume on him? (Matthew 26:6-13)

Why is it important to be open to what God wants instead of our own view of what is practical or good?

3   Judas arranges to betray Jesus

How did Jesus' opponents get their opportunity to arrest Jesus? (Matthew 26:14-16)

4   The Last Supper

What was the significance of Jesus' Last Supper with the disciples? (Matthew 26:17-30; John 13:1-17)

Why should we remember Jesus' Last Supper?

5   The Garden of Gethsemane

What do you notice about Jesus and his disciples in the garden of Gethsemane? (Matthew 26:31-46)

What does this incident teach you about prayer and God's will?

6 The betrayal and arrest of Jesus

How was Jesus arrested? (Matthew 26:47-56)

What does it mean to betray or desert Jesus?

7 Jesus' trial before Caiaphas

What is noteworthy about Jesus' trial before the high priest? (Matthew 26:57-68)

When is it better to say nothing than to defend yourself?

8 Peter's denial

What human tendencies do you see in Peter's denial of Christ? (Matthew 26:69-75)

How do believers today deny Christ, whether they realize it or not?

In summary, what have you learned about Jesus' commitment to the Father's will?

What have you learned about your own commitment to God's will?

YOUR WALK WITH GOD

Bible

Read Matthew 27 three times, noting observations and applications.

Prayer

Day One: Adoration—Read Isaiah 53, then write a prayer of adoration, worshipping God for the gift of his Son.

Day Two: Confession—Take a look back over the last month of your life. List the sins you remember being guilty of committing. List the acts of obedience you have been guilty of *not* doing. Confess these to God.

Day Three: Thanksgiving—Go over your list of confessions and write "Paid in full" next to every sin. Thank God for forgiving each and every sin and for accepting you through his grace.

Scripture Memory

Going a little farther, he fell with his face to the ground and prayed, "My Father, if it is possible, may this cup be taken from me. Yet not as I will, but as you will."   Matthew 26:39

The theme of the next study is the crucifixion and death of Jesus. To prepare for the study, complete the assignment found in the On Your Own section.

ON YOUR OWN

Note: You will need to complete the following assignment before you come to the next meeting.

It is the first century A.D. You are a reporter for the *Jerusalem Gazette*. You have been assigned by your editor to go out and get the real story on Jesus. You are to list accurately all the details found in Matthew 27. But because you readers want more than the facts, you have to explain to them the significance of the facts you uncover. In other words, they want to know, "Why is this important?"

Take a piece of paper and divide it into two columns (shown below). List the facts on the left and your thoughts, insights, and applications on the right. Try to come up with at least four key facts and observations from Matthew 27.

Facts of the Story   **Insights and Applications**

10

The Crucifixion

Christ's death is one of the most important topics you can study as a Christian. More than just a painful death, the Crucifixion was Christ's act of paying for *your sins.* He was mocked, humiliated, and rejected in paying for *your* guilt. It is easy to think of Christ's death only as an event that happened in the past. But if it weren't for Christ's death, your life today would not be what it is.

As you read the story of Christ's death, imagine the scenes in your mind—see the soldiers' dirty faces, hear their sarcastic taunts, feel the marketplace heat, imagine the thorns digging into Jesus' head, and so on. Try to imagine what it must have been like for Jesus to go through the suffering he faced. Put yourself right next to it all.

In this study, you will learn about the price Jesus paid—the suffering and humiliation he endured for your benefit.

STUDY

Reporting the Facts

Turn to your assignment from the previous study. As a reporter, what two facts and observations from the account in Matthew 27 were most striking to you?

Jesus' Public Humiliation

What do you remember as one of your most painful experiences of rejection?

What are some of the specific sufferings that Jesus endured at his public trial? (Matthew 27:11-26)

How did the soldiers cause Jesus to suffer? (Matthew 27:27-31)

What emotions do these scenes evoke in you?

Jesus' Suffering on the Cross

What sufferings did Jesus endure on the cross? (Matthew 27:35-50)

What emotions does this scene evoke in you?

What was most significant to you about Jesus' death on the cross?

Jesus' Death and Burial

What events happened right after the Crucifixion? (Matthew 27:51-66)

BOTTOM LINE

YOUR WALK WITH GOD

Bible

Read Matthew 28 three times.

Prayer

Day One: Adoration—Write a prayer in answer to the question, "What if Jesus had not been raised from the dead?" For example: "Father, if Jesus had not been raised from the dead, I _____ and you _____." Or: "Lord, I worship you for the resurrection of Jesus, because otherwise _____."

Day Two: Confession—In what specific ways do you demonstrate a lack of faith—perhaps a worry that you need to entrust to God? Confess this and pray that God will increase your faith.

Day Three: Supplication—Pray by name for three unsaved friends.

Scripture Memory

But God demonstrates his own love for us in this: While we were still sinners, Christ died for us. Romans 5:8

Our next study will focus on the Resurrection. Why is this event central to Christianity? How do our Easter celebrations highlight or miss this important event?

ON YOUR OWN

Read and study the account of the resurrection of Jesus in each of the Gospels:

Matthew 28:1-15

Mark 16:1-14

Luke 24:1-49

John 20:1-31

What facts appear in all four Gospel accounts?

What facts appear in at least two of the Gospel accounts? (List which Gospels contain each fact.)

What facts appear in only one Gospel account?

The Resurrection

PURPOSE

In our secular culture, Easter lives in the shadows of other holidays. Compared to Christmas, for example, Easter hardly makes an appearance. In most churches this is not the case, but for the vast majority of modern men and women, Easter comes and goes without much fanfare.

Yet Christ's resurrection is a pivotal event. It is absolutely central to the Christian faith. You could not be a Christian without it being true. Our salvation stands or falls with the resurrection of Jesus. Without the Resurrection, Christianity is just one more religion. The Resurrection declares that faith in Christ is a personal encounter with the living God, not just a philosophy, a set of morals, or the teachings of a spiritual leader. The Resurrection declares the deity of Jesus Christ, God among us, all-powerful and triumphant over sin. It tells us that God came, took away our sins, and invited us to receive forgiveness.

In this study, we will focus our attention on what makes the Resurrection so significant.

STUDY

The Resurrection is recorded in all four Gospels: Matthew 28:1-15; Mark 16:1-14; Luke 24:1-49; John 20:1-31. Turn to the assignment you prepared for this study to answer the questions below.

Jesus Rose from the Dead

What facts appear in all four Gospel accounts?

What do we gain from having four different accounts of this event?

The Significance of the Resurrection

What makes the Resurrection significant to our faith? (1 Corinthians 15:12-19)

What implications does Christ's resurrection have for our understanding about life after death? (1 Corinthians 15:29-32, 35-54)

How does the Resurrection give us hope?

How does Christ's death on the cross and his resurrection especially touch you?

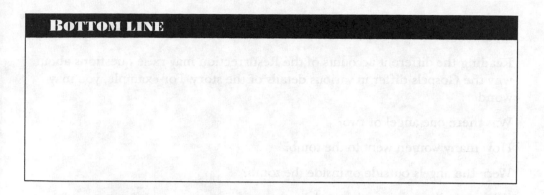

YOUR WALK WITH GOD

Bible

Read Acts 1 three times.

Prayer

Day One: Adoration—From your memory of all you've learned in *"Follow Me!"* make a list of all that the praiseworthy deeds Jesus did as a man on earth. Praise him for his deeds.

Day Two: Confession—Ask God to bring to mind sins of which you have not been aware, and confess these to him.

Day Three: Supplication—Continue to pray for your three unsaved friends.

Scripture Memory

Therefore, my dear brothers, stand firm. Let nothing move you. Always give yourselves fully to the work of the Lord, because you know that your labor in the Lord is not in vain. 1 Corinthians 15:58

In the next study we will take a closer look at Jesus' final words to his followers—the Great Commission. What do you think Jesus wanted to impress upon his disciples at that point?

Reading the different accounts of the Resurrection may raise questions about why the Gospels differ in various details of the story. For example, you may wonder:

Was there one angel or two?

How many women went to the tomb?

Were the angels outside or inside the tomb?

Who actually went into the tomb?

Did Peter go *into* the tomb, or just look in?

Those kinds of questions may lead to deeper ones:

Why didn't God cause the writers to report the details exactly alike?

Isn't the Bible infallible and inerrant?

How can we explain the apparent contradictions between the Gospels?

The following three principles may help you as you ponder such questions.

1 Differences from one narrative to another arise because each writer left out some details.

A true contradiction between the Gospel accounts is actually harder to find than you might think. For example, does John's comment in John 20:1 that Mary Magdalene went to the tomb, with no mention of any other women going with her, rule out the possibility that other women were with her but just not mentioned? Not at all. His story doesn't really contradict the others—it just doesn't say everything. We have a hint of this in John 20:2, where Mary says "we"; even in John there's a hint that she was not alone.

In other words, facts left out of one account but not another do not necessarily indicate a contradiction between the two. A true contradiction would be a statement such as, "And Mary Magdalene came early to the tomb alone—no one was with her." No such contradictory statements exist in the Gospels.

Consider the following story. A woman was waiting for a bus with a friend. As the bus approached, the crowd pressed forward and she was pushed in the path of the bus. The bus struck her and an ambulance was called. Meanwhile, the friend called the woman's husband and told him, "Your wife has been hit by a bus. I'll call you when we find out what hospital she's been taken to." About an hour later, the husband received another call. This time it was a police officer. "I'm sorry to inform you Sir, but your wife has just been killed in a car accident." When the man expressed his shock that he had heard her injuries from being hit by the bus were not that severe, the officer replied that there was no bus involved and that she had been killed while a passenger in an automobile.

From the looks of the above story, the police officer and the friend are contradicting each other. Somebody is mistaken on what vehicles were involved and the nature of the woman's injuries (or else one or both of those people called the wrong husband!). In any event, if we were reading this account in two different newspapers (one story from the officer and one story from the friend) it is hard not to assume the accounts are mixed up. If you read those stories, you'd want to ask some more questions to find out what really went on.

As it turns out both the friend and the police officer were one hundred percent correct in every detail. The woman had been hit by a bus. Before the ambulance arrived, a passerby offered to take her to the hospital. While en route in that car, the woman was involved in the fatal auto accident. The two stories can be completely harmonized omitting nothing. Had someone tampered with either story to erase the contradiction, the final story would not have been true to the actual events. So leaving the stories as they are, even with apparent contradictions, is a more honest and credible option. That is how the Gospels come to us. In many cases they can be made to complement each other without negating each other.

2   Differences often authenticate a story because they prove there has been no attempt to change the details in order to harmonize the accounts.

When faced with a possible contradiction, even generally honest people may fudge some of the details to make stories fit. This is especially true of dishonest people. But in the New Testament we don't see this adjusting going on—the writers told their stories as they saw them (or heard them).

And as we said above, the contradictions may not turn out to be real contradictions after all.

3   Scripture is God-breathed, and God is incapable of falsehood.

We say the Bible is without error because any book from God (as fulfilled prophecy and its incredible trustworthiness show that it is) would have to be utterly and completely truthful. God cannot lie, nor can he mix truth with error. And if God says something through a prophet, it will always and in every case be true because God is speaking and he cannot speak falsely.

No prophet speaking by God's Spirit ever uttered a falsehood. "No prophecy of Scripture came about by the prophet's own interpretation. For prophecy never had its origin in the will of man, but men spoke from God as they were carried along by the Holy Spirit" (2 Peter 1:20-21). If the Scriptures are God's Word, they contain no errors.

What then should we do when we come upon an apparent contradiction or mistake? We recognize them as such and try to solve them. Harmonize the accounts or admit we don't know. But one option we don't have is to impute error to God. Once we say that God inspired error, we open the door to anything in the Bible being a possible mistake. If God ever told one lie, he could have told a thousand. But our God never has, and never will, tell us something that isn't true. That is why difficulties in Scripture don't change its inerrancy, because we anchor our hope of pure truth in his nature and recognize that such problems will ultimately have a solution.

Jesus had this view of Scripture. A quick survey of the Gospels will reveal his tremendous respect for its truth. Statements such as, "The Scripture cannot be broken" (John 10:35), and, "Since you do not believe what [Moses] wrote, how are you going to believe what I say?" (John 5:47) show his trust in and high view of the operation of God's Spirit in the Bible.

If Jesus is Lord of our lives, he is Lord of our beliefs. And he believed in the invulnerability and utter truthfulness of Scripture; to call him Lord then is to agree with him about the nature of the Bible.

The accounts of Jesus' resurrection do differ. But their apparent contradictions are really just that—apparent. Our finite minds will have to wait for a full disclosure of details that will resolve all our questions. But based on who God is and in submission to the authority of Christ, we do not impute error to God, and we fully anticipate the answer to our every question that will show God's complete and eternal truthfulness.

The Call
(Great Commission)

12

PURPOSE

Remember when people used to ask you, "What do you want to be when you grow up?" Whatever your answer to that question when you were younger, you probably had *some* reply. Even if you didn't have specific plans for the future, you knew that eventually you would become an adult. One day you would grow up.

To grow up is a mixed blessing. Adulthood brings new responsibilities as well as new opportunities. Not only can you do more, you're *expected* to do more. And like all change, adulthood brings you to more uncharted territory, making you unsure exactly what lies ahead. It's the same with being a Christian.

From among his many followers, Jesus chose twelve men to be with him all the time. It's true that he did this so they could learn for themselves, but there was also another reason: so they could learn how to teach others. Jesus wanted his disciples not only to become godly men, but also to become teachers of others. That meant, eventually, becoming disciple-makers themselves.

Jesus wants every Christian to mature to the point of making disciples. That means growing from a place of mere belief to that of persuading others to believe; helping new believers understand their faith; and encouraging other believers to follow him. In other words, following Jesus means passing on the faith to others—what is often called fulfilling the Great Commission.

In this study, we will explore what it means to fulfill the Great Commission.

The Call

The Scene: Imagine that you are the owner and president of a dynamic, medium-size company with about 50 employees. It's Tuesday night, about 8:30 P.M. You're sitting in your favorite living room chair. It's your first real moment today to rest and relax with your spouse. The work day is behind you and the kids are in bed. The phone rings and you reach to get it . . .

You: Hello?

Caller: Hello, is _____ there?

You: Yes, this is _____.

Caller: Are you sitting down?

You: Well, as a matter of fact I am.

Caller: That's good, because what I have to tell you may surprise you. This is the president of the United States calling.

You: Oh, sure it is . . . and I'm the Queen of England! Come on, who is this really?

Caller: This is no prank call. This is your president, and I am very serious about this. If you don't believe me, just look out your front door. You will find two men standing there in dark suits. They are Secret Service agents, and they will show you IDs if necessary.

You: OK, I'll check—and let me add, they had better be there.

(You go to the front door. Sure enough, two men in dark suits are standing there, just as he said. You ask for their IDs, and they show them. Suddenly you realize you have been rude to the president of the United States and have left him on hold! You rush back and pick up the receiver.)

You: Mr. President, I'm sorry, really . . . I just never expected in a million years to hear from you!

President: I understand.

You: What can I do for you, Sir?

President: Please listen. I have a matter of grave importance to communicate to you.

You: I'm all ears, Mr. President. Go ahead.

President: There is an issue of national security and world peace at stake and, though you may find this hard to believe, you are the only one—let me repeat that, the only one—who can help. The future of our country and the world is hanging in the balance. I need you. We need you. The world needs you. Do you want me to continue.

You: Oh yes, Mr. President, anything I can do for my country.

President: I am glad you are willing. I cannot stress enough that you are the only one we can count on.

You: I understand, Mr. President. What can I do?

President: We need you to go on a mission, a top secret mission. You will not know where you are going until you are at the Air Force base awaiting takeoff.

You: It sounds very exciting, sir. Tell me more.

President: Well, there is one major catch, and as we see it, no way around it.

You: What's that, Sir?

President: The mission will take ten years, during which you will be completely unable to contact any friends or loved ones.

You: Wow! That is a catch!

President: We will give you one year to prepare yourself, your family, and your business for your absence. Your departure date is set for one year from today. I will have my people get in touch with you to help you in any way possible. Please plan carefully and thoughtfully, as you will have no contact with the life you now have for ten years. You will receive a packet of information shortly with all the necessary details. I will also call back to see how preparations are going. Until then, thank you. The world will perhaps never know just how significant a role you played in its destiny.

If you were this business owner, what would you do to ensure that the corporation maintains the same superior performance in your absence?

How Jesus Made Disciples

1 Focused on a Few

How many disciples did Jesus train closely? (Mark 3:14-19)

2 Selected Them Carefully

How did Jesus choose the twelve with whom he worked closely? (Luke 6:12-13)

3 Trained Them

Why did Jesus choose the Twelve? (Mark 3:13-14)

What purpose did Jesus have in sending his disciples out to preach? (Mark 3:13-14)

What final mission did Jesus give his twelve disciples? (Matthew 28:18-20)

What tasks does this "Great Commission" require of all Christians living today? (Matthew 28:18-20)

How can your unique gifts and abilities be used in making disciples for Christ?

Life Dedicated to the Great Commission

1 Home

In what ways can you disciple your family?

2 Church

In what way can you be a disciple-maker in your local church?

3 Friends

What coworkers, neighbors, or friends can you serve as Christ's messenger?

4 World

In what ways do you think discipling others will eventually impact the world?

What is one change you could make in your life to better fulfill Jesus' call to make disciples?

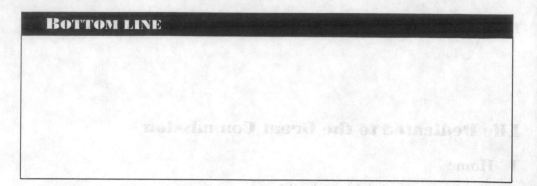

YOUR WALK WITH GOD

Bible

Read Acts 2 three times, noting observations and applications.

Prayer

Day One: Adoration—Make a list of the truths about Jesus that have changed your life in some way.

Day Two: Confession—Ask God to forgive any hardness or insensitivity you may have had toward Christ.

Day Three: Supplication—Write out a prayer of devotion to Jesus, asking God to make you a better follower each day.

Scripture Memory

Review the following verses: Matthew 26:39; Romans 5:8; 1 Corinthians 15:58.

The next study will be a review of the book. Take a look back through the pages of this study guide and think about the most important insights you have gained, and how these truths have impacted your life.

13

Reviewing "Follow Me!"

This review culminates your study of *"Follow Me!"* the third book in the *Walking With God Series*. Use this time to reflect on your experience and to summarize what you've learned about following Jesus.

As you know by now, following Christ is more than just a matter of believing in Jesus. It is a personal relationship with him, involving prayer, worship, and trust. This review invites you to look back on what you've learned over the last twelve weeks and apply it to that ongoing relationship.

Discoveries about Following Jesus

During the past twelve weeks, what has been your most meaningful insight about following Christ?

What does it mean to do everything to the glory of God?

What is one area of your life that you have submitted to the lordship of Christ as a result of this study?

What are some ways a Christian should serve Christ with money and possessions?

What are some benefits you receive as a result of following Jesus?

How have you had to adjust your expectations of God?

In what way does opposition to your faith challenge you?

What do you need to do to ready yourself for Jesus' return?

What about doing God's will do you find most difficult?

What is most meaningful to you about Christ's death?

Why is it significant that Jesus rose from the dead?

What can you do at this time in your life to help fulfill the Great Commission?

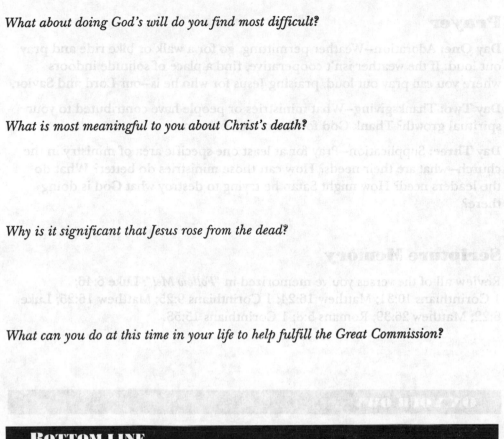

BOTTOM LINE

YOUR WALK WITH GOD

Bible

Read the book of Mark through in order to capture a sense of Jesus' life and its life-changing, world-changing, history-changing, and eternity-changing impact.

Prayer

Day One: Adoration—Weather permitting, go for a walk or bike ride and pray out loud. If the weather isn't cooperative, find a place of solitude indoors where you can pray out loud, praising Jesus for who he is—our Lord and Savior.

Day Two: Thanksgiving—What ministries or people have contributed to your spiritual growth? Thank God for them each by name.

Day Three: Supplication—Pray for at least one specific area of ministry in the church—what are their needs? How can those ministries do better? What do the leaders need? How might Satan be trying to destroy what God is doing there?

Scripture Memory

Review all of the verses you've memorized in *"Follow Me!"*: Luke 6:46; 1 Corinthians 10:31; Matthew 16:24; 1 Corinthians 9:25; Matthew 16:25; Luke 6:22; Matthew 26:39; Romans 5:8; 1 Corinthians 15:58.

ON YOUR OWN

Self-Evaluation

Your group leader will be meeting with you to discuss your current spiritual condition and your hopes for growing in your faith. Please take some time to reflect honestly on where you stand right now within these four basic categories of Christian growth. Rate yourself in each category.

+   **Doing well. I'm pleased with my progress so far.**

✓   **On the right track, but I see definite areas for improvement.**

—   **This is a struggle. I need some help.**

A Disciple Is One Who . . .

Walks with God

To what extent is my Bible study and prayer time adequate for helping me walk with God?

Rating:

Comments:

Lives the Word

To what extent is my mind filled with scriptural truths so that my actions and reactions show I am being transformed?

Rating:

Comments:

Contributes to the work

To what extent am I actively participating in the church with my time, talents, and treasures.

Rating:

Comments:

Impacts the world

To what extent am I impacting my world with a Christian witness and influence?

Rating:

Comments:

Other issues I would like to discuss with my small group leader:

The *Walking With God Journal* is the perfect companion to the *Walking With God Series.* Use it to keep your notes during Bible study, record your prayers, or simply jot down your thoughts and insights. (0-310-91642-9)

NOTES

NOTES

NOTES

NOTES

NOTES

NOTES

NOTES